In memory of my friend,
Douglas Graham

ΣΚΗΝΗ·ΠΑΣ·
Ο·ΒΙΟΣ·ΚΑΙ·Π
ΑΙΓΝΙΟΝ··Η·
ΜΑΘΕ·ΠΑΙΖΕ
ΙΝ·ΤΗΝ·ΣΠΟ
ΥΔΗΝ·ΜΕΤΑ
ΘΕΙΣ·Η·ΦΕΡΕ·
ΤΑΣ·ΟΔΥΝΑΣ

The Magic Wood

A POEM BY HENRY TREECE

PAINTINGS BY BARRY MOSER

Willa Perlman Books · HarperCollins Publishers

THE MAGIC WOOD

The wood is full of shining eyes,
The wood is full of creeping feet,
The wood is full of tiny cries:
You must not go to the wood at night!

I met a man with eyes of glass
And a finger as curled as the wriggling worm,
And hair all red with rotting leaves,
And a stick that hissed like a summer snake.

The wood is full of shining eyes,
The wood is full of creeping feet,
The wood is full of tiny cries:
You must not go to the wood at night!

He sang me a song in backwards words,
And drew me a dragon in the air.
I saw his teeth through the back of his head,
And a rat's eyes winking from his hair.

The wood is full of shining eyes,
The wood is full of creeping feet,
The wood is full of tiny cries:
You must not go to the wood at night!

He made me a penny out of a stone,
And showed me the way to catch a lark
With a straw and a nut and a whispered word
And a pennorth of ginger wrapped up in a leaf.

The wood is full of shining eyes,
The wood is full of creeping feet,
The wood is full of tiny cries:
You must not go to the wood at night!

He asked me my name, and where I lived;
I told him a name from my Book of Tales;
He asked me to come with him into the wood
And dance with the Kings from under the hills.

The wood is full of shining eyes,
The wood is full of creeping feet,
The wood is full of tiny cries:
You must not go to the wood at night!

But I saw that his eyes were turning to fire;
I watched the nails grow on his wriggling hand;

And I said my prayers, all out in a rush,
And found myself safe on my father's land.

The wood is full of shining eyes,
The wood is full of creeping feet,
The wood is full of tiny cries:
You must not go to the wood at night!

The poem "The Magic Wood" was originally published in a collection of poems by Henry Treece under the title *The Black Seasons*, published by Faber & Faber, copyright 1945. It also appeared in *Collected Poems* by Henry Treece, published by Alfred Knopf, copyright 1946.

The Magic Wood
Text copyright © 1992 by The Estate of Henry Treece
Illustrations copyright © 1992 by Barry Moser
Printed in the United States of America.
All rights reserved.
ISBN 0-06-020802-3. — ISBN 0-06-020803-1 (lib. bdg.)
Library of Congress Catalog Card Number 91-29547
1 2 3 4 5 6 7 8 9 10
First Edition

The text for Henry Treece's "The Magic Wood" was composed in Matthew Carter's Galliard Bold and Galliard Bold Italic by Linoprint Composition Co., Inc., New York, New York. The paintings were executed in ink and transparent watercolor on paper handmade by Simon Green at the Barcham Green Mills, Maidstone, Kent, Great Britain. The calligraphy is the work of Reassurance Wunder. The transparencies were made by Gamma One Conversions, New York, New York, and the color separations by Imago Ltd, Hong Kong. The entire book was printed by Worzalla Publishing Company, Stevens Point, Wisconsin, on 80# Lustro Dull made by the S.D. Warren Company. Production by John Vitale and Danielle Valentino. Designed by Barry Moser and Christine Kettner.